*Learning about Cats*

# THE
# ABYSSINIAN CAT

by Joanne Mattern

**Consultant:**
Bruce Dickinson
President
Abyssinian Cat Club of America

CAPSTONE BOOKS
an imprint of Capstone Press
Mankato, Minnesota

Capstone Books are published by Capstone Press
151 Good Counsel Drive, P.O. Box 669, Mankato, Minnesota 56002
http://www.capstone-press.com

*Library of Congress Cataloging-in-Publication Data*

Mattern, Joanne, 1963–
The Abyssinian cat/by Joanne Mattern.
    p.cm.—(Learning about cats)
    Includes bibliographical references (p. 45) and index.
    Summary: Discusses the history, development, habits and care of Abyssinian cats.
    ISBN 0-7368-0564-8
    1. Abyssinian cat—Juvenile literature. [1. Abyssinian cat. 2. Cats. 3. Pets] I. Title.
II. Series.

SF449.A28 M38 2001
636.8'26—dc21                                                                                      00-025667

**Editorial Credits**
Angela Kaelberer, editor; Linda Clavel, cover designer and illustrator; Katy Kudela,
    photo researcher

**Photo Credits**
Ginger S. Buck, 34
International Stock/Tetsu Yamakazi, 10, 12
KAC Productions/Greg W. Lasley, 8, 37, 38
Linda Kay Weber, 19
Norvia Behling, 6, 15, 16, 24, 27, 28, 30, 32
Ron Kimball/Ron Kimball Studios, cover, 4, 20, 40–41
Root Resources/Laurie Myhre-Choate, 22

1  2  3  4  5  6  06  05  04  03  02  01

# Table of Contents

## Quick Facts about the Abyssinian

### Description

**Size:**  Abyssinian cats have long, slender bodies. They are medium-sized cats.

**Weight:**  Adult Abyssinians weigh 7 to 12 pounds (3.2 to 5.4 kilograms).

**Physical features:**  Abyssinians are long, slim cats. They have short, thick coats. They have wedge-shaped heads. Their eyes and ears are large.

| | |
|---|---|
| **Color:** | Abyssinian cats' coats can be one of several colors. The most common are red, blue, fawn, and ruddy. Abyssinians' coats are ticked. This means each hair has light and dark bands of color. |

## Development
| | |
|---|---|
| **Place of origin:** | The Abyssinian breed may be from Abyssinia. This region of Africa now is the country of Ethiopia. |
| **History of breed:** | The Abyssinian is believed to be one of the oldest natural domestic cat breeds. Natural breeds began without much interference from cat breeders. A cat that may have been an ancestor of today's Abyssinian was brought to Europe in 1868. |
| **Numbers:** | In 1999, the Cat Fanciers' Association (CFA) registered 1,962 Abyssinians worldwide. Owners who register their Abyssinians record the cats' breeding records with an official club. The CFA is the world's largest organization of cat breeders. |

# Chapter 1

## The Abyssinian Cat

The Abyssinian is an active, intelligent, and friendly breed. People often call these cats "Abys."

### Appearance

Abyssinians are medium-sized cats. Adult Abys weigh 7 to 12 pounds (3.2 to 5.4 kilograms). Abys have long, slender, and muscular bodies. Their heads are shaped like a triangle or wedge. Abys have large eyes and ears.

Abyssinians are shorthaired cats. Their thick fur is soft and sleek.

Abyssinians have ticked coats. This means that each hair on an Abyssinian's body is marked with bands of light and dark color.

**Abyssinians' coats have a ticked pattern.**

**Many Abyssinians seem to enjoy water.**

This ticked pattern is common in wildcats such as cougars or lions. This ticking makes the Aby look more like wildcats than other cat breeds do.

## Personality
Abyssinians seem to enjoy being around people. They tend to stay near their owners.

They seem to want to be involved in all of their owners' activities. But they rarely sit on people's laps or want to be held.

Abys are natural athletes. They often run, jump, and climb. They also are more playful than many cat breeds.

Abyssinians are quiet cats with soft voices. They communicate their needs to their owners through sounds and movements.

Abyssinians often climb. Owners often find them sitting in high places such as the tops of bookcases or refrigerators.

Most cats do not like to get wet. But many Abys seem to enjoy water. They may play with water that drips from sink or bathtub faucets.

The Abyssinian's friendly, playful nature makes it an especially good pet for families with children. Abyssinians also get along well with dogs and most other cats. But Abys do not like crowds. These cats do not seem happy in households with many other animals.

*Chapter 2*

# Development of the Breed

The Abyssinian gets its name from the African region of Abyssinia. Today, this country is called Ethiopia.

No one is sure where or when the Abyssinian breed began. Some people think that these cats lived in the palaces of the Egyptian pharaohs. These kings ruled Egypt thousands of years ago. Mummified cats have been discovered in ancient Egyptian tombs. A drying process preserved these cats' bodies after death.

Statues and drawings of cats found in Egyptian tombs look much like today's Abyssinian. These cats have slender bodies, wedge-shaped heads, and large eyes. But these features also are found in the

Statues of ancient Egyptian cats look much like today's Abyssinian.

**Abyssinians' ticked coats look similar to rabbit fur.**

Oriental cat breed. No one can prove exactly what kind of cat lived in ancient Egypt.

### The Abyssinian Arrives in Europe

During the 1860s, British soldiers fought a war in Abyssinia. In Abyssinia, these soldiers saw cats with ticked coats.

In 1868, a British Army officer brought a cat named Zula back to Great Britain. A woman named Mrs. Captain Barrett-Leonard bought Zula from the officer. Zula had a ticked coat. But otherwise, she looked little like today's Abyssinian cats.

Some people believe Zula may have been the founder of the Abyssinian breed. Others believe that the breed began in Great Britain. British breeders crossed striped silver and brown tabby cats with ticked cats native to Great Britain. These cats were known as "bunny" cats. Their fur color was similar to that of rabbit fur.

Other people believe that the Abyssinian breed began in Southeast Asia. Traders may have brought these cats to Great Britain.

Great Britain's National Cat Club registered its first Abyssinians in 1896. British breeders exhibited a few Abyssinians in cat shows during the late 1800s.

## The Modern Abyssinian
The early 1900s were difficult for the Abyssinian breed. Great Britain and other European nations were involved in two world wars. These wars were World War I (1914–1918) and World War II (1939–1945). Most people did not have the time

or money to breed cats during the war years. During that time, many Abys also died of a disease called feline leukemia (FeLV). This disease attacks cats' immune systems. It leaves the cats unable to fight off infections and other illnesses. The Abyssinian breed almost disappeared in Europe. The breed did not reach large numbers again until the 1960s.

The breed also developed slowly in North America. During the early 1900s, some breeders brought Abyssinian cats to North America from Europe. But the breed did not become popular in North America until the 1930s. At that time, breeders brought several Abyssinians from Great Britain to the United States.

By the 1950s, many North American breeders were raising Abyssinians. Today, the Abyssinian is more popular in North America than it is in Europe. Each year, the Abyssinian ranks as one of the top five cat breeds in North America.

**The Abyssinian ranks as one of the top five cat breeds in North America each year.**

# Chapter 3

# Today's Abyssinian

$M$any people consider the Abyssinian to be one of the most graceful and elegant cat breeds. People often exhibit these cats in cat shows. But not every Abyssinian can compete in these shows.

## Breed Standard

Judges look for certain physical features when they judge Abyssinians in cat shows. These features are called the breed standard.

The breed standard says the Abyssinian cat should be medium-sized. Its body should be long and muscular. The short, ticked fur should lie close to the body. An Abyssinian cat's head should be shaped like a triangle or wedge. Its ears should be large and pointed. Its eyes should be almond shaped and large. The

**An Abyssinian's eyes can be either gold or green.**

eyes can be either gold or green. A thin, dark line should circle the eyes.

An Aby's coat is an important part of the breed standard. An Aby's coat should be shiny and bright in color. Its ticking must be clear and even all over its body. The original Abyssinian coat color was ruddy. This coat is dark brown with black ticking. Over the years, breeders developed other colors.

Today, four colors meet the breed standard. These are ruddy, red, blue, and fawn. Red Abys have orange-red fur with brown ticking. Blue Abys are light blue-gray with darker blue-gray ticking. Fawn Abys have light pink-beige fur with brown ticking.

Breeders also have developed silver, chocolate, and lilac Abys. Silver Abys have silver coats with black ticking. Chocolate Abys are a medium brown color with black ticking. Lilac Abys have pink-gray coats with darker pink-gray ticking. But these colors are rare. Abyssinians of these colors do not meet the breed standard. They cannot be exhibited in most cat shows.

**Red Abyssinian cats have orange-red fur with brown ticking.**

Other features can prevent an Abyssinian from being exhibited in cat shows. One is white fur on any part of the body except around the nose, chin, and upper throat. Another is a reverse ticking pattern in the coat. Cats with this ticking pattern have darker coats

**The Somali breed began with longhaired Abyssinian cats.**

with lighter ticking. But Abyssinians that are not of show quality still make good pets.

## Somalis

All Abyssinian cats have short fur. But they carry a gene for long fur. Genes are parts of cells that parents pass to their offspring. Genes determine how the offspring will look. A longhaired kitten sometimes will be born in a litter of Abyssinians. At first, breeders did not know what to do with these kittens. Longhaired Abyssinians could not be exhibited in cat shows.

In the 1960s, some breeders began to breed these longhaired cats. These longhaired Abys now are called Somalis. They are named after the African country of Somalia. This country borders Ethiopia.

Somalis have ticked coats and features similar to Abyssinians. But their fur is longer. They also have thick, bushy tails. By the late 1960s, the Somali was considered a separate breed from the Abyssinian. All North American cat associations allowed Somalis to be exhibited in cat shows by the late 1970s.

# Chapter 4

# Owning an Abyssinian

People can adopt Abyssinians in several ways. They may contact breeders, pet stores, animal shelters, or breed rescue organizations.

An Abyssinian can sell for several hundred dollars. Abyssinians tend to have fewer kittens per litter than other cat breeds. Most of these kittens are male. This means that there are fewer female cats to breed and produce kittens. These facts can make Abyssinians more expensive than other cat breeds.

## Abyssinian Breeders

People who want a show-quality Abyssinian should buy one from a breeder. Most breeders carefully select their cats for breeding. They breed cats that have the best features. The parents are likely to pass these features to the

People who want a show-quality Abyssinian should buy one from a breeder.

**People who buy Abyssinian kittens from breeders often can meet the kittens' parents.**

kittens. A person who buys a kitten from a breeder often can meet the kitten's parents. This gives owners an idea of how the kitten will look and behave as an adult.

Many Abyssinian breeders live in the United States and Canada. People who want to find a local Abyssinian breeder can attend cat shows. Cat shows are good places to talk to breeders and see their cats. People also should ask breeders for references to contact. Other people who have bought cats from the breeders can act as references. These people can describe their experiences with the breeders.

Breeders also advertise in newspapers and cat magazines. These ads are organized by breed. They list the names, addresses, and phone numbers of breeders. Breeders also may have Internet sites.

## Pet Stores

People also can buy Abyssinians at pet stores. Pet stores may have Abys for sale or may be able to get them from local breeders.

Many pet stores are clean and sell healthy animals. But people should check out stores before they buy a pet. Buyers should visit stores and ask store workers where they get their animals. Buyers should look closely at the pet store animals to make sure they look healthy and alert. The animals' cages should be large, comfortable, and clean. The animals also should have plenty of food, fresh water, and toys.

## Animal Shelters

Many people adopt cats from animal shelters. These places keep unwanted animals and try to find homes for them.

An animal shelter can be a good place to adopt a cat for several reasons. Owners who adopt a pet from an animal shelter may save the pet's life. Many more animals are brought to shelters than there are people available to adopt them. Animals that are not adopted often are euthanized. Shelter workers euthanize animals by injecting them with substances that stop their breathing or heartbeat.

Animal shelters also can be a less expensive way to adopt a pet. Most shelters charge only a small fee. Some veterinarians provide discounts on medical services for shelter animals.

There also can be some problems involved in adopting an animal from a shelter. Shelters often have mixed-breed pets available for adoption instead of purebred pets such as Abyssinians. People interested in adopting an Aby can contact a shelter. They can ask shelter workers to contact them when an Aby is brought to the shelter.

**People sometimes can adopt Abyssinian cats from animal shelters.**

Another problem with shelter animals is that their histories often are unknown. Shelter workers usually do not know anything about the animals' parents, health, or behavior. Some owners may adopt cats with medical or behavioral problems. Shelter cats also seldom have papers showing that they are registered with official cat organizations. Owners who do

not have registration papers for their cats cannot exhibit them in cat shows.

## Breed Rescue Organizations

People interested in adopting a purebred Abyssinian may want to contact a breed rescue organization. These organizations are similar to shelters in some ways. Breed rescue organization members find unwanted or neglected animals. They care for the animals and try to find new owners to adopt them. People usually can adopt the animals for a small fee.

Breed rescue organizations are different from shelters in some ways. They usually rescue just one breed. They rarely euthanize animals. Animals from breed rescue organizations usually are purebred. They even may be registered.

People can find information about breed rescue organizations in several ways. These organizations often have their own Internet sites. They may advertise in cat magazines. Local animal shelters also may have information about breed rescue organizations.

**Purebred Abyssinians may be available from breed rescue organizations.**

*Chapter 5*

# Caring for an Abyssinian

Abyssinians are strong, healthy cats. With good care, Abys can live 15 or more years.

## Indoor and Outdoor Cats

Some cat owners allow their cats to roam outdoors. This practice is not safe. Cats that roam outdoors have much greater risks of developing diseases than cats that are kept indoors. Outdoor cats also face dangers from cars and other animals.

Owners of indoor cats need to provide their cats with a litter box. Owners fill the boxes with small bits of clay called litter. Cats eliminate waste in these litter boxes. Owners should clean the waste out of the box each day and change the litter often. Cats are clean animals. They may refuse to use a dirty litter box.

**Outdoor cats face dangers from disease, cars, and other animals.**

**31**

**Abyssinians do well on a diet of high-quality dry or moist cat food.**

Both indoor and outdoor cats need to scratch. Cats mark their territories by leaving their scent on objects they scratch. Cats also scratch to release tension and keep their claws sharp. This habit can be a problem if cats choose to scratch on furniture, carpet, or curtains. Owners should provide their cats with scratching posts. They can buy scratching posts at pet stores or make them from wood and carpet. Cats seem to prefer scratching posts covered with a rough material such as indoor/outdoor carpet.

## Feeding

Abyssinians need a high-quality diet. Most pet foods available in supermarkets or pet stores provide a balanced, healthy diet.

Some cat owners feed dry food to their cats. This food usually is less expensive than other types of food. Dry food also can help keep cats' teeth clean. It will not spoil if it is left in a dish.

Other owners feed moist, canned food to their cats. This type of food should not be left out for more than an hour. It will spoil if left out too long.

Cats need to drink fluids to stay healthy. Owners should make sure their cats always have fresh, clean water available. Most cats like the taste of milk. But milk can upset adult cats' stomachs.

## Grooming and Nail Care

An Abyssinian's short, sleek coat requires little care from owners. Most cats do a good job

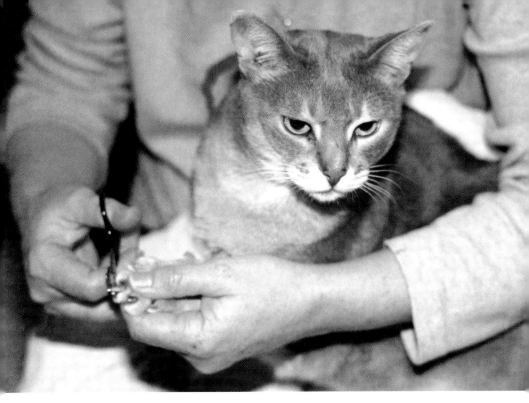

**Owners should trim Abyssinians' nails every few weeks.**

grooming their fur with their tongues. An occasional brushing will remove loose hair. Owners also can rub their Abyssinians with a damp cloth to keep the cats' coats shiny.

The tip of a cat's claw is called the nail. Cats need their nails trimmed every few weeks. This helps reduce damage if cats scratch on carpets or furniture. Trimming also protects cats from infections caused by ingrown nails.

Infections can occur when a cat does not sharpen its claws often. The claws then grow into the pad or bottom of the paw.

It is best to begin trimming a cat's nails when it is a kitten. The kitten will become used to having its nails trimmed as it grows older. Veterinarians can show owners how to trim their cats' nails with a special nail clipper.

## Dental Care

Abyssinians need regular dental care to protect their teeth and gums from plaque. This coating of bacteria and saliva causes tooth decay and gum disease. Dry cat food helps remove plaque from cats' teeth. Owners also should brush their cats' teeth at least once a week. They can use a special toothbrush made for cats or a soft cloth. They also should use a toothpaste made for cats. Owners should never use toothpaste made for people. Cats may become sick if they swallow it.

Brushing may not be enough to remove the plaque from older cats' teeth. They may need to have their teeth cleaned once each year by a veterinarian.

## Health Problems

Most Abyssinians are healthy. But some do develop serious diseases. Some Abys suffer from a kidney disorder called renal amyloidosis. Other cat breeds also can get this disease.

Renal amyloidosis is an inherited disease. Inherited diseases are passed down from the cats' parents. Good cat breeders test their animals for inherited diseases if a test is available. No test for renal amyloidosis has been developed for living cats.

## Veterinarian Visits

Abyssinians must visit a veterinarian regularly for checkups. Most veterinarians recommend yearly visits. Older cats may need to visit a veterinarian two or three times per year. More frequent checkups will help a veterinarian spot any health problems in older cats.

An owner who adopts an Abyssinian should make a checkup appointment as soon as possible. The veterinarian will check the Aby's heart, breathing, internal organs, eyes, ears, mouth, and coat.

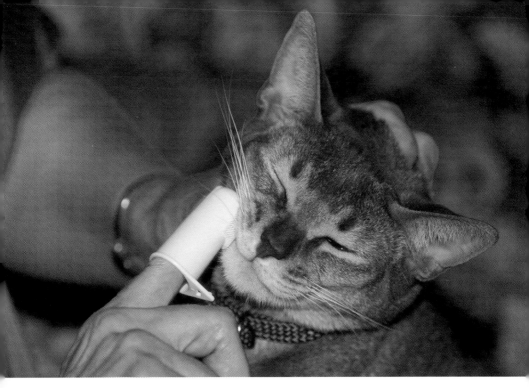

**Owners can use a special toothbrush made for cats to brush Abyssinians' teeth.**

The veterinarian also will give vaccinations to the Aby. These shots of medicine help prevent serious diseases. These diseases include rabies, feline leukemia, and feline panleukopenia. Rabies is a deadly disease that is spread by animal bites. Most states and provinces have laws that require owners to vaccinate their cats against rabies. Feline panleukopenia also is known as feline

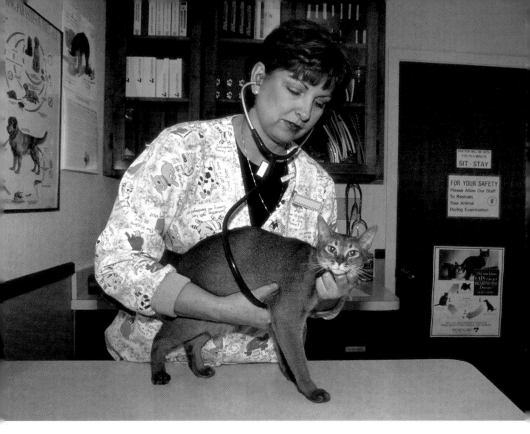

**Abyssinians should have regular checkups with a veterinarian.**

distemper. This disease causes fever, vomiting, and eventual death. Cats also can receive vaccinations for several respiratory diseases that cause breathing or lung problems.

Some vaccinations are given each year. Some are given less often. Cats that are kept indoors do not always need all vaccinations.

Breeders have information on which vaccinations Abys need. Owners should keep a record of their cats' vaccination dates. This record helps owners be sure that their cats have received all the vaccinations that they need.

Veterinarians also spay female cats and neuter male cats. These surgeries make it impossible for cats to breed. All cats should be spayed or neutered unless their owners want to breed them. The surgeries keep unwanted kittens from being born. They also help prevent diseases such as infections and cancers of the reproductive organs.

Spayed and neutered cats usually have calmer personalities than cats that are not spayed or neutered. They also are less likely to wander away from home to find mates.

Regular visits to a veterinarian are an important part of cat ownership. Owners and veterinarians can work together to help Abyssinians live long, healthy lives.

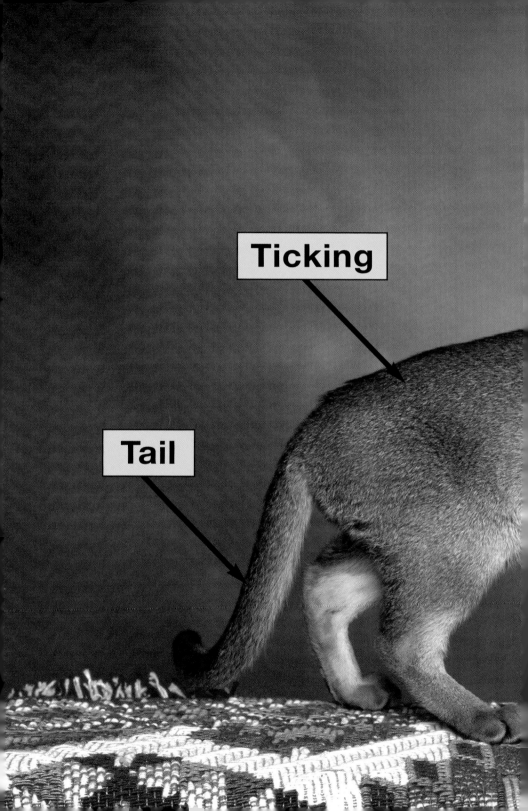

# Quick Facts about Cats

A male cat is called a tom. A female cat is called a queen. A young cat is called a kitten. A family of kittens born at one time is called a litter.

**Origin:** Shorthaired cat breeds descended from a type of African wildcat called *Felis lybica*. Longhaired breeds may have descended from Asian wildcats. People domesticated or tamed these breeds as early as 1500 B.C.

**Types:** About 40 domestic cat breeds exist. The Cat Fanciers' Association recognizes 33 of these breeds. The smallest breeds weigh about 5 to 7 pounds (2.3 to 3.2 kilograms) when grown. The largest breeds can weigh more than 18 pounds (8.2 kilograms). Cat breeds may be either shorthaired or longhaired. Cats' coats can be a variety of colors. These colors include many shades of white, black, gray, brown, and red.

**Reproduction:** Most cats mature at 9 or 10 months. A sexually mature female cat goes into estrus several times each year. Estrus also is called "heat." During this time, she can mate with a male. Kittens are born about 65 days after breeding. An average litter includes four kittens.

**Development:** Kittens are born blind and deaf. Their eyes open about 10 days after birth. Their hearing develops at the same time. They can live on their own when they are 6 weeks old.

**Life span:** With good care, cats can live 15 or more years.

**Sight:**  A cat's eyesight is adapted for hunting. Cats are good judges of distance. They see movement more easily than detail. Cats also have excellent night vision.

**Hearing:**  Cats can hear sounds that are too high for humans to hear. A cat can turn its ears to focus on different sounds.

**Smell:**  A cat has an excellent sense of smell. Cats use scents to establish their territories. Cats scratch or rub the sides of their faces against objects. These actions release a scent from glands between their toes or in their skin.

**Taste:**  Cats cannot taste as many foods as people can. For example, cats are not very sensitive to sweet tastes.

**Touch:**  Cats' whiskers are sensitive to touch. Cats use their whiskers to touch objects and sense changes in their surroundings.

**Balance:**  Cats have an excellent sense of balance. They use their tails to help keep their balance. Cats can walk on narrow objects without falling. They usually can right themselves and land on their feet during falls from short distances.

**Communication:**  Cats use many sounds to communicate with people and other animals. They may meow when hungry or hiss when afraid. Cats also purr. Scientists do not know exactly what causes cats to make this sound. Cats often purr when they are relaxed. But they also may purr when they are sick or in pain.

# Words to Know

**breeder** (BREED-ur)—someone who breeds and raises cats or other animals

**estrus** (ESS-truss)—a physical state of a female cat during which she will mate with a male cat; estrus also is known as "heat."

**euthanize** (YOO-thuh-nize)—to painlessly put an animal to death by injecting it with a substance that stops its breathing or heartbeat

**neuter** (NOO-tur)—to remove a male animal's testicles so that it cannot reproduce

**spay** (SPAY)—to remove a female animal's uterus and ovaries so that it cannot reproduce

**ticking** (TIK-ing)—bands of light and dark color on a hair

**vaccination** (vak-suh-NAY-shun)—a shot of medicine that protects a person or animal from disease

**veterinarian** (vet-ur-uh-NER-ee-uhn)—a doctor who is trained to treat the illnesses and injuries of animals

# To Learn More

**Fogle, Bruce.** *The Encyclopedia of the Cat.* New York: D K Publishing, 1997.

**Helgren, J. Anne.** *Abyssinian Cats: Everything about Acquisition, Care, Nutrition, Behavior, Health Care, and Breeding.* Hauppauge, N.Y.: Barron's, 1995.

**Kallen, Stuart A.** *Abyssinian Cats.* Checkerboard Animal Library. Edina, Minn.: Abdo & Daughters, 1995.

**Stone, Lynn M.** *Abyssinian Cats.* Read All about Cats. Vero Beach, Fla.: Rourke, 1999.

**Track, Judah.** *Guide to Owning an Abyssinian Cat.* Popular Cat Library. Philadelphia: Chelsea House Publishers, 1999.

You can read articles about Abyssinian cats in *Cat Fancy* and *Cats* magazines.

# Useful Addresses

**Abyssinian Cat Club of America (ACCA)**
6236 Lakeview Drive
Falls Church, VA 22041

**Canadian Cat Association (CCA)**
220 Advance Boulevard
Suite 101
Brampton, ON L6T 4J5
Canada

**Cat Fanciers' Association (CFA)**
P.O. Box 1005
Manasquan, NJ 08736

**The International Cat Association (TICA)**
P.O. Box 2684
Harlingen, TX 78551

**Somali/Abyssinian Breed Rescue
& Education (S.A.B.R.E.)**
P.O. Box 838
Cary, IL 60013

# Internet Sites

**Abyssinian Cat Club of America (ACCA)**
http://website.lineone.net/~mikkaraby/acca

**American Veterinary Medical Association
    Presents—Care for Pets**
http://www.avma.org/care4pets

**Canadian Cat Association (CCA)**
http://www.cca-afc.com

**Cat Fanciers' Association (CFA)**
http://www.cfainc.org

**The International Cat Association (TICA)**
http://www.tica.org

**Somali/Abyssinian Breed Rescue
    & Education (S.A.B.R.E.)**
http://www.sabrecats.org

# Index